STRANGERS and SOJOURNERS with Me

(Lev.25:23)

One of the figures that recurs throughout the Scriptures is that of a tent. We shall see as our study progresses, that the present creation as set forth in Genesis 1 is limited; the heaven above is likened to a tent which will be folded up and put away when the conflict of the ages ends. The figure of a tent dweller is not limited to any one calling, it is true of Israel, it is true of the Church. In addition, it is even said that God, in fellowship with the redeemed, and in the person of His Son shares this limitation of a tent, and, during the ages, walks and wars and shares the hardships associated with a campaign. Let us make sure of this encouraging feature, before we prosecute our studies further.

In Leviticus 25 the law of the sabbatic year and the law of the Jubilee is announced, followed by the practical observation that a man's possession, which for any reason he has sold, decreases in price as the year of Jubilee approaches. Then comes the great revelation of Leviticus 25:23:

> "The land shall not be sold for ever: (in perpetuity, absolutely or beyond recovery, *Companion Bible* note), for the land is Mine; for ye are strangers and sojourners with Me" (Lev.25:23).

What this means for God to say "with Me", can be gathered from similar statements recorded elsewhere. Abraham had been promised the land of Palestine, and had walked through the length and breadth of it from the river of Egypt unto the great river Euphrates, and this territory included the land of the Hittites (Gen.15:18-21). This promise was given to Abraham "In the same day" that he had been told that his seed should be a "stranger in a land that is not theirs" and should be afflicted four hundred years (Gen. 15:13). Abraham too, to whom the promise was made, was to go to his fathers and be buried in a good old age (Gen.15:15). In Genesis 23 we find Abraham mourning for the death of Sarah, and speaking to the sons of Heth (i.e. Hittites, see verse 10). Instead of saying to the sons of Heth, "God has already given me this land, which includes the land of the Hittites, and therefore I demand access to the cave of Machpelah as my right", he says:

"I am a stranger and a sojourner with you" (Gen. 23:4).

and paid "as much money as it is worth". This, a burying place, is the only "possession" Abraham had in the land of promise! Without the general overall pattern of the Scriptures, and the fact that all the redeemed are involved in the battle of the ages, Abraham's attitude could be misconstrued as an act of unbelief, whereas, Hebrews 11 says:

"By faith he *sojourned* in the land of promise *as in a strange country*, dwelling in tabernacles (i.e. tents) with Isaac, and Jacob, the heirs with him of the same promise" (Heb.11:9).

In 1 Chronicles 29 we have a similar confession made by David. This time the possession of the *land* is not in view but the building of the *temple*. Earlier in the story we learn that David had said "See now, I dwell in an house of cedar but the ark of God dwelleth within curtains" (2 Sam.7:2), and although Nathan the prophet at first concurred with the project, he was told by God to say to David:

"Shalt thou build Me an house for Me to dwell in? Whereas I have not dwelt in any house since the time that I brought up the children of Israel out of Egypt, even to this day, but have walked in a tent and in a tabernacle. In all the places wherein I have walked with all the children of Israel spake I a word with any of the tribes of Israel whom I commanded to feed My people Israel, saying, Why build ye not Me an house of cedar?" (2 Sam.7:5-7).

Subsequently we learn that Solomon, David's son, would build an house for God and that Solomon recognised the dispensational reason why David his father was not permitted to exchange the tent for the temple, saying to the king of Tyre:

"Thou knowest how that David my father could not build an house unto the name of the Lord his God for the wars which were about him on every side, until the Lord put them under the soles of his feet. *But now* (note the dispensational change) the Lord my God hath given me rest on every side, so that there is neither adversary nor evil occurrent" (1 Kings 5:3,4).

Let us note the conditions expressed here. David could not build

    (a)   for the wars "on every side"

    (b)   until enemies were under the soles of his feet.

Solomon could build:

    (a)   for he now had rest "on every side"

    (b)   and no adversary (Heb. *Satan*).

Hebrews 2 looks forward to the day when the Saviour shall have "all things under His feet" and 1 Corinthians 15 looks forward to the day when the last enemy shall be destroyed, but as in the case of David, Hebrews 2 says:

"But now we see not yet all things put under Him"

but instead, the Saviour Who is yet to triumph gloriously is seen made a little lower than the angels for the suffering of death.

In 1 Chronicles 22, David calls his son Solomon and says:

"My son, as for me, it was in my mind to build an house unto the name of the Lord my God: but the word of the Lord came to me, saying, Thou hast shed blood abundantly, and hast made great wars: thou shalt not build an house unto My name" (1 Chron. 22:7,8).

In all this it is evident that while there is a war on, the people of God will be tent dwellers, even as God has said of Himself. So in 1 Chronicles 29, where once again the building of the temple is in view, we meet the words "strangers and foreigners":

"For we are strangers before Thee, and sojourners, as were all our fathers: our days on the earth are as a shadow, and there is none abiding" (1 Chron. 29:15).

3

"For thus saith the high and lofty One that inhabiteth eternity, Whose name is Holy;

(a)   I dwell in the high and holy place,

(b)   with him also that is of a contrite and humble spirit" (Isa. 57:15).

"In all their afflictions He was afflicted" (Isa. 63:9).

"When thou passest through the waters, I will be with thee" (Isa. 43:2).

Abraham said to the Hittites:

"I am a stranger and a sojourner *with you*" (Gen.23:4).

David said to the Lord:

"We are strangers *before Thee*, and sojourners" (1 Chron. 29:15).

The Lord said to Israel:

"Ye are strangers and sojourners *with Me*" (Lev. 25:23).

Having established this one blessed fact that the Lord Himself shares the restrictions and inconveniences that must ever accompany a state of war, let us examine the two words "stranger" and "sojourner". The Hebrew word translated "stranger" in Leviticus 25:23 is *ger*, embodied in the name Moses gave his son Gershom:

"For he said, I have been a stranger in a strange land" (Exod.2: 22).

The first occurrence of this word is found in Genesis 15:13:

"Thy seed shall be a stranger in a land *that is not theirs*",

the second occurrence being uttered by Abraham in the very land of promise, when he said to the sons of Heth:

"I am a stranger and a sojourner with you" (Gen.23:4).

These two occurrences encompass the meaning of the word in Scripture.

(1)   Literally strangers, because in a land not theirs.

(2)   Spiritually strangers, because, "here we have no continuing city, but we seek one to come".

The word translated "sojourner" in Leviticus 25:23 is the Hebrew word *toshab* derived from *yashab* "to dwell"; in this case one who dwells rather as an emigrant than as a native with full rights. The attitude of the spiritual sojourner is expressed in Deuteronomy 2:26-28:

> "And I sent messengers out of the wilderness of Kedemoth unto Sihon King of Heshbon with words of peace, saying, Let me pass through thy land: I will go along by the high way, I will neither turn unto the right hand nor to the left. Thou shalt sell me meat for money, that I may eat; and give me water for money, that I may drink: only I will pass through on my feet".

The Tent, and the Six Days Creation

When the Lord said to His people:

> "Ye are strangers and sojourners *with Me*",

more than a somewhat far-fetched sympathy was implied.

When He said:

> "In all the places wherein I have walked with all the children of Israel spake I a word ... saying, Why build ye not Me an house of cedar?

the reference was not only back to the erection of the Tabernacle in the wilderness, but to the six days creation, when the submerged earth was restored and refitted for the advent of Adam, the man made in the image of God.

On the second day of that re-creating work, we read:

> "And God said 'Let there be a firmament ... and God called the firmament heaven'" (Gen.1:6-8).

With very few exceptions, this limited "heaven" is the only one referred to in the Scriptures. Once now and again it is recognized that there is a heaven far above the present firmament, as for example Solomon's confession:

> "Behold the heaven and the heaven of heavens cannot contain Thee" (1 Kings 8:27).

The word "firmament" found its way into the A.V. because of the great influence the Latin Vulgate had upon Biblical phraseology. This in its turn was an attempt to translate the Greek of the Septuagint which reads *stereoma*. The LXX in its turn attempted to translate the Hebrew word *raqia*, which the margin of the A.V. at Genesis 1:6 gives as *expansion*, and refers to Exodus 39:3; Numbers 16:39 and 2 Samuel 22:43. Exodus 39:3 speaks of beating gold "into thin plates". Numbers 16:39 speaks of the brazen censers that were made into broad plates for a covering for the altar, while 2 Samuel 22:43 reads:

> "Then did I beat them as small as the dust of the earth, I did stamp them as the mire of the street, and did spread them abroad" (Heb. *raqia*).

What this "stretched out" firmament means spiritually can be seen in the Psalms and in Isaiah. Psalm 104:2 speaks of God "Who stretches out the heavens like a curtain" but does not give any reason, or supply a hint of purpose. This Isaiah does. In Isaiah 40:22 we read of God that He is the One that:

> "Stretcheth out the heavens *as a curtain*, and
>
> Spreadeth them out *as a tent*, to dwell in".

Here we have the Divine purpose in the making of the "firmament"; it suggests that for the working out of the purpose of the Ages, God Himself leaves His High Glory, and shares the limitations of a pilgrim life, "dwelling in a tent" as did Abraham, Isaac and Jacob (Heb.11:9), walking with Israel through the wilderness, and living with them in the tabernacle, a symbol that the goal of the ages was not yet attained, or the warfare of the ages over.

At first sight there seems little to connect the tabernacle and the wilderness with war, and it will be therefore incumbent upon us to give some place to its consideration.

＊＊＊＊＊＊＊

The Camp of the Saints

When we read of "the camp of the saints" in Revelation 20:9 it is pardonable if we associate it with that state of peace which is linked with "the feast of tabernacles", but if we examine the way in which the word translated "camp" is used, we shall have the full authority that comes from using "the words which the Holy Ghost teacheth".

The Greek word translated "camp" is *parembole*. In six out of ten occurrences, it is translated "castle" (Acts 21: 34,37; 22:24; 23:10,16,32). Here we have no peaceful, idyllic camp, but a castle with soldiers and centurions, captains and chains, and all the associations of military preparedness and iron strength. The word occurs three times in Hebrews, once translated "armies" (Heb.11:34), and twice "camp". It is used of "saints" and of "aliens". The LXX uses, in the majority of instances, the Hebrew word *machaneh*, which meets us for the first time in Genesis 32:2 where we read "This is God's host". The word is used in Exodus 14: 9 and 24 of Pharaoh's army, with its horses and chariots. The book of Numbers devotes several chapters to the formation of the Camp of Israel, and the words of Numbers 1:3 "all that are able to go forth to war in Israel" are repeated thirteen times in this one chapter. This is the "camp" of Israel, a warlike disciplined company, with the tabernacle and its ministering families in the midst (Num.2:17).

We return with this added information to Genesis 1:6 and to Isaiah 40:22, with this solemn yet wonderful thought. The catastrophe indicated in Genesis 1:2 is echoed in Jeremiah 4:23-27, and in Isaiah 34:11. The wording of Jeremiah speaks for itself, but the reader may not know that "without form and void" is in view in the words "confusion" (*tohu* without form) and "emptiness" (*bohu* void). These are the words which the Holy Ghost useth, and we are enjoined to compare spiritual things with spiritual (1 Cor.2:13). Unless we are going to teach that the Holy Spirit has intentionally employed the identical words of Genesis in Isaiah and in Jeremiah to *deceive us*, the conclusion is inescapable. Genesis 1:2 indicates "The Lord's vengeance" (Isa.34:8) and is answered in the future by the day that is coming when "All the host of heaven shall be dissolved, and the heavens shall be rolled together as a scroll" (Isa.34:4; Heb.1:11 and 2 Pet.3:10). Scripture makes it clear that some angels fell (2 Pet.2:4; Jude 6) and that the Devil sinneth "from the beginning" (1 John 3:8). It is also very clearly stated that there will be a future "war in heaven" in which Michael and his angels will fight against the dragon and his angels (Rev. 12:7-9) upon the casting down of whom, a loud voice in heaven announces the coming of the kingdom of God. Hebrews 2:5 suggests that a past world had been put in subjection to angels, and from all that can be gathered it appears that God chose this earth to be the battle ground on which should be fought out to a finish this conflict between light and darkness, and that the construction of a limited heaven in Genesis 1:6 was intended to keep the conflict within bounds, this tent stretched overhead remaining until the day spoken of by Peter (2 Pet.3:10). If we may borrow the sentiment put into the mouth of King Henry V by Shakespeare, where that mortal and earthly king is said to have "laid by" his majesty "and plodded like a man of working days" until victory was achieved, so the Lord says to us in the Scriptures, while this war is on, I lay aside My glory, I "tabernacle" (John 1:14) among you, I share the common soldier's lot, I know the sleepless night, the weariness, the hardship and the comradeship of the battle field. I am a "stranger and sojourner" with you ("like a man of working days" for the word sojourner is developed from the word *jour* a day), I too will be a tent dweller until the victory is attained, I too will refrain and limit Myself, "I will not drink of the fruit of the vine until I drink it new in My Father's kingdom". This figure of a tabernacle as applied to the present limited creation is further impressed upon us by a word employed by the Creator Himself when expostulating with His servant Job:

"Where wast thou when I laid the foundation of the earth? ... Whereupon are the foundations thereof fastened?" (Job 38:4-6).

The challenging word here is the word translated "foundation" in verse 6, for the Hebrew word is translated some fifty times "sockets" when Moses described the tabernacle in the wilderness. "Curtains, tent, the true tabernacle, and sockets" are used alike of the Tabernacle in the wilderness and of the present Creation with its temporary heaven.

8

Pilgrims and Strangers

We have been obliged to make a detour, in order that the reader should be in possession of the evidences now before him, that this "Tent-dwelling" is by no means an accidental, but an integral part of the Scriptural picture of the character of the present life of the believer who would walk with his God. We now return to our original quest.

If the reader were asked what is the first consequence revealed in Exodus 12 of the Passover, he may not without the preparation already supplied, put his finger on the fact that the moment a person is redeemed, he becomes *ipso facto* a Pilgrim.

"And thus shall ye eat it:

(1) With your loins girded,

(2) Your shoes on your feet, and

(3) Your staff in your hand, and

(4) Ye shall eat it in haste,

It is the Lord's Passover" (Exod.12:11).

This is entirely foreign to the Biblical custom for partaking of a meal. Loins girded speak of readiness for work, shoes were left at the door and the feet washed before reclining at the table. No one in the ordinary way would think of dining with staff in hand, and it is an extraordinary admonition to be told "to eat in haste", but all is seen in true perspective if the pilgrim character is intended.

It surely is no accident, that the first station after Israel left Rameses in Egypt is called "Succoth" or "Booths" (Exod.12:37), for it was enacted in the law, that this fact should be remembered annually at the Feast of Tabernacles:

"Ye shall dwell in booths seven days ... that your generations may know that I made the children of Israel to dwell in booths, when I brought them out of the land of Egypt" (Lev.23:42,43; Neh. 8:14-17).

The word "tabernacle" in the title "The Feast of Tabernacles" is the Hebrew word *succoth* (Young's Concordance *sokkah*).

9

Hebrews 11 contains much that illuminates the teaching of the Scriptures regarding the Pilgrim character of the believer. We will reserve the evidence of Hebrews 11:1 until we deal with the symbolism of 2 Corinthians 5:1-8, and come immediately to the reference to Abraham.

> "By faith he sojourned in the land of promise, as in a strange country, dwelling in tabernacles with Isaac and Jacob, the heirs with him of the same promise. For he looked for a city which hath foundations, whose builder and maker is God" (Heb.11:9, 10).

A few verses further on, this pilgrim character is again brought forward with fuller emphasis:

"These all died in faith

(1) Not having received the promises,

(2) But having seen them afar off, and

(3) Were persuaded of them, and embraced them, and

(4) Confessed that they were strangers and pilgrims in the earth.

(5) For they that say such things declare plainly that they seek a country, and truly

(6) If they had been mindful of that country from whence they came out,

(7) They might have had opportunity to have returned.

(8) But now they desire a better country, that is, an heavenly:

(9) Wherefore God is not ashamed to be called their God;

(10) For He hath prepared for them a city" (Heb.11:13-16).

We have set out this passage in ten sections, in the hope that each step in this wonderful argument will be more readily recognised.

It strikes one as strange at first to speak of "faith" *not* receiving the promises, but the second step shows the reason, they were *afar off*, and so although having no concrete evidence here and now of their calling and hope, such were *persuaded*, and not only so, they *embraced* them, thereby *confessing* that they were *pilgrims* and *strangers* in the earth. Such without speaking a word "declare plainly" that they seek a country.

The word translated pilgrim in Hebrews 11:13 is *parepidemos*, from *para* "beside", *epi* "on" and *demos* "people", and indicates a person who is not a permanent resident, but lives as a stranger, often without citizen rights. Those to whom Peter wrote his first epistle would know something of this relationship, for he addressed them as "strangers, scattered throughout Pontius Galatia, etc." (1 Pet.1:1). The word translated "stranger" in Hebrews 11:13 is the Greek word *xenos*, used by Paul in Ephesians 2:12 and 19. In 1 Peter 2:11 we have the two titles used together:

"Dearly beloved, I beseech you as strangers and pilgrims, abstain from fleshly lusts which war against the soul"

here the word "stranger" translates the Greek word *paroikos* which in its verbal form is rendered "sojourning" in 1 Peter 1:17; while the word translated "pilgrim" here is the Greek *parepidemos* translated in 1 Peter 1:1 "stranger". A mechanical system of translation would put these words in fetters and say "pilgrim" must be used always for one Greek word, and "stranger" for the other. The flexible translation of the A.V. gains far more than it sacrifices. For a believer becomes a "stranger" because he is a pilgrim passing on to the heavenly city. Conversely the believer becomes a "pilgrim" because by reason of the essential separating character of redemption (see margin of Exod.8:22,23) he finds himself a "stranger" in the earth. This attitude of heart and its consequences is brought forward at the close of Hebrews:

"Jesus ... suffered without the gate.

Let us go forth therefore unto Him without the camp, bearing His reproach.

For here we have no continuing city,

But we seek one to come" (Heb.13:12-14).

No "continuing" city. The Apostle has already touched upon this aspect, saying in Hebrews 12:27:

"And this word, Yet once more, signifieth the removing of those things that are shaken, as of things that are made, that those things which cannot be shaken may remain, or *continue*".

There can be no such thing as "a continuing city" in such

a state, "bearing His reproach". Once again, this looks back to what has already been said:

"Ye endured ... reproaches and afflictions"(Heb.10:32,33), and the great renunciation of Moses, in his "refusing" "choosing" and "esteeming" (Heb.11:24-26). The sequel being "Knowing ... ye have in heaven a better and an enduring substance", where the word "enduring" is the same as that translated "continuing" already referred to. There is more however. Hebrews 13:14 adds "They seek one to come". This harks back to Hebrews 11:14 where we read:

"For they that say such things declare plainly that they seek a country".

Such have no need to plaster their cars with pennants, advertising to the passer by, that they have been to this and that city. They have no need for badges, or buttonholes, their whole being "declares plainly" their true objective, "They seek a country". "Seeking" is an index of character (Matt.6:32,33; Luke 12:29-31; Phil.2:21; Col.3:1). Again, Hebrews 13:14 contrasts the city that does not continue with "one to come" (*mello*). This again is a key word:

"The world to come" (Heb.2:5; 6:5).

"Good things to come" (Heb.9:11; 10:1; 11:20).

"Should after receive" (Heb.11:8).

One corrective word must be brought forward. Hebrews 13:13 *does not say* "Let us go forth without the camp" as it is sometimes misquoted, it says "Let us go forth *unto Him* without the camp" which is vastly different. We do not become "Pilgrims and Strangers" because we are cranks, or because we are misanthropic, because we suffer from liver troubles, or because we pride ourselves Pharisaically on our peculiar separateness from the common man. We go *unto Him*. This somewhat lengthy diversion seemed called for as we follow the lead of the inspired writer in his expansion of what is implied and involved in Abraham willingly becoming a "tent dweller".

The A.V. uses the word "tabernacle" in Hebrews 11:9, but this is altered to read "tent" in the R.V. The glorious colouring and the golden furniture of the Tabernacle in the

12

wilderness, colours our ideas of Abraham's choice, and misleads us. Abraham exchanged a highly civilized city life, Ur of the Chaldees, for the inconvenience of a "moving tent" not a "tabernacle" in our present conception of the term. The O.T. words translated "tabernacle" are the Hebrew words:

ohel   "A tent" (Gen.4:20; 12:8; Exod.26:11).

mishkan   "A dwelling" from shaken "to dwell" (Gen.14:13; Exod. 25:8).

This word gives us the expression "The Shekinah glory", a term borrowed from Rabbinical literature. Sok "a booth" hence the place named "Succoth" and its connection with the feast of Tabernacles. Israel, as we have already reminded the reader, kept the feast of "Tabernacles" to keep in mind the fact that they had previously dwelt in "booths". It may come as a shock to some, to learn that where the Apostle was refreshed at the place called "Three Taverns" the word in the original is tabernai, for a "tabernacle" or a "tavern" was originally a "temporary booth erected for the refreshment of travellers and pilgrims". It has no immediate association with the sale of strong drink, that has come about through the process of time and custom. The N.T. word translates the Greek word skene which means a tent. Instead therefore of raising Abraham's "tent" to the dignity and glory of the "Tabernacle" of Exodus 25, we should reverse our thinking and marvel that the God of glory should condescend to become "a tent dweller" as He has reminded us in 2 Samuel 7:6 "I have walked in a tent (ohel) and in a tabernacle (mishkan). The idea of "walking" here is suggestive of the continually moving tent rather than a settlement.

"The Word was made flesh" (John 1:14).

The testimony of Scripture concerning the coming of our Saviour in the flesh, is that He left a glory and riches and position that is beyond our comprehension, and humbled Himself by taking upon Him human nature:

13

"For ye know the grace of our Lord Jesus Christ, that, though He was rich, yet for your sakes He became poor, that ye through His poverty might be rich" (2 Cor.8:9).

This must be remembered when we read in John 1:14:

"The Word was made flesh and dwelt among us"

where the word "dwelt" is "tabernacled" or "became a tent dweller". Moffatt has caught the essence of this passage, translating it:

"So the Logos became flesh and tarried among us".

When first we read of the "gold, silver and brass, and blue and purple, and fine linen" we forget that the eye of the ordinary Israelite never saw the inside of the Tabernacle; what he saw was a tent, with a covering of badger skins, and this is a truer type of John 1:14.

Following the words "The Word was made flesh and dwelt (as in a tent) among us" the Apostle continued:

"And we beheld His glory" (John 1:14).

We gather from Isaiah 53:2,3 that to the unbelieving eye He appeared to have no form nor comeliness, and the only glimpse of His supernal glory that was vouchsafed during the Lord's earthly life, was upon the mount of Transfiguration. We know from John 17 that the Lord had a glory "before the world was", but after His condescension and incarnation He speaks of a glory that was "given" Him, and that He had given to His disciples (John 17:5,22). This was a glory which they could "behold" (John 17:24), and yet in 1 Timothy 6:14-16 we learn that He has a glory which no man "hath seen" in the past, nor "can see" in the future. What kind of glory, then, did the Apostles see?

"We beheld His glory, the glory as of the only begotten of the Father, full of grace and truth" (John 1:14).

The words "glory", "Father" and "Only-begotten" are *anarthrous* i.e. without the article "the", and Moffatt has observed this in his translation which reads:

" ... glory such as an only Son enjoys from his father".

"The glory referred to by the Apostle here in 1:14 is rather the kind of glory that is compatible with the status of being an only begotten one of a father" (*Life Through His Name* page 51).

This special aspect of the Saviour's glory is further defined and limited by the words "Full of grace and truth".

Uninstructed by the Scriptures, we might have expected "Fulness" to be linked with "The Word, Who was God" or "Who made all things" but this is not so. This fulness can be shared by the believer and is associated by contrast with the ministry of Moses. The blessed truth that underlies this apparent difficulty is found in the fact, that the Saviour first of all "Emptied Himself" (Phil.2:7) for so *ekenose* means, and then, as the One Mediator, and for our sakes He could be filled with all the fulness of God. *Pan to pleroma* "all the fulness" is used alike of the believer (Eph.3:19 see also 1:23 and Col.1:19; 2:9,10). The innate and uncreated glory of God can be shared by none. This, in John 1:14 is essentially "the glory of the Only begotten". Parallel with John 1:18 is Colossians 1:15-19. No "fulness" is mentioned in connection with "the Firstborn of all creation" but only with "The Firstborn from the dead" (Col.1:18,19). As the Firstborn of all Creation the Lord still was far above us, but as the Firstborn of the Father (and of Mary His mother Matt.1:23) He became "Jesus" or "Emmanuel" God with us. Contrary to the ways of the world, to which the cross is both foolishness and weakness (1 Cor.1:18,25), it is through His *poverty* that we are made rich (2 Cor.8:9).

We return with this most wondrous revelation of Divine love to John 1:14 and consider the words "Full of grace and truth". John and the epistle to the Hebrews use the word "True" not only as an opposite of"False" but as the opposite of "Type and shadow". The True light, True worshippers, True bread, the True vine, the True tabernacle, "Figures of the True". Hebrews 9:24 tells us that the Holy places made by hands were "the figures or antitypes of the true, namely

Heaven itself". In like manner, the Lord acknowledged that Israel received manna in the wilderness, but that He was "the True, the antitypical bread".

We return to John 1:14 and read "Full of true, i.e. antitypical grace"; Gospel grace instead of legal shadow. This interpretation is necessitated, moreover, by the words that follow "Grace for grace".

> "For the law was given by Moses, but grace and truth came by Jesus Christ" (John 1:16,17).

The preposition *anti* used in the phrase "grace for grace" sets one sort of grace *over against* another, and the context tells us that the one sort of grace is found in the shadows and types of the law of Moses, but that "True grace", Gospel grace, is found only in Jesus Christ. In this is His fulness, and in this we share.

The Tabernacle

If the body of flesh and blood of the Saviour could be described as a tabernacle or a tent, so also can the body of the believer. Peter says:

> "Yea, I think it meet, as long as I am in this tabernacle, to stir you up by putting you in remembrance; knowing that shortly I must put off this my tabernacle, even as our Lord Jesus Christ hath showed me" (2 Pet.1:13,14).

This tabernacle or tent is something *in* which Peter could be thought to be, and which he would *put off* or *lay aside* at his death. Peter knew that he would not inhabit "this tent" for ever, saying "as long as I am in this tabernacle", but nevertheless could at the same time "look for new heavens and a new earth" after the greater tabernacle or tent had been dissolved (2 Pet.3:11). These notes turn our attention to 2 Corinthians 4, where the reference is clearly to the present body of flesh and blood. The second epistle to the

Corinthians speaks more than once of the Apostle's consciousness of his own human frailty.

"We were pressed out of measure, above strength, insomuch that we despaired even of life: but we had the sentence of death in ourselves, that we should not trust in ourselves, but in God which raiseth the dead" (2 Cor.1:8,9).

"We have this treasure in earthen vessels, that the excellency of the power may be of God, and not of us" (2 Cor.4:7).

"For which cause we faint not; but though our outward man perish, yet the inward man is renewed day by day" (2 Cor.4:16).

In this last reference, the inward man corresponds with Peter's reference to himself, while the outward man corresponds with "this tent" which he inhabits for "so long" but which he could ultimately "put off", and this in accord with what the Lord Jesus had showed him (John 21:18,19). The "renewing" (*anakainoo*) is referred to in Colossians:

"Ye have put off the old man with his deeds; and have put on the new man, *which is renewed* in knowledge after the image of Him that created him" (Col.3:9,10).

This "renewing" (*anakainosis*) is the renewing of the mind (Rom.12:2), and follows regeneration (Tit.3:5). After a reference to "things not seen" allying this passage with Hebrews 11, 2 Corinthians adopts the figure of the tent, or tabernacle:

"For we know that if our earthly house of this tabernacle were dissolved, we have a building of God, an house not made with hands, eternal in the heavens" (2 Cor.5:1).

It is important to notice the way the Genitive is used here, "our earthly house of this tabernacle" is not good English. This is an instance of Genitive of Apposition, and the English idiom requires the words "that is to say" to give equivalent sense:

"For we know that if our earthly house, *that is to say*, this tabernacle or tent were dissolved".

In contrast with the "earthly house", we have one "in the heavens". In contrast with the dissolution of the one, we are told that the other is eternal. In contrast with the flimsy nature of a "tent" we have (a) "a building" (b) "of God"

17

(c) "an house not made with hands". The fact that the resurrection body of the believer is not "made with hands" shows, if we translate Hebrews 9:11 correctly, that it is "not of this creation"; the word "building" of the A.V. is changed to read "creation" in the R.V., *ktisis* being correctly translated in 2 Corinthians 5:17 by the word "creature". The resurrection body of the believer belongs to the new creation. During this earthly pilgrimage "we groan" and share the groan of a suffering creation around us (Rom.8:22). We ourselves also, that have the firstfruits of the spirit groan within ourselves, waiting for the adoption, to wit, the redemption of our body (Rom.8:23). Nor is this all, we have already learned that the Lord has identified Himself with us in our sojourning, and so we read yet once more, in Romans 8 of One who "groans", this time the Spirit who helps our infirmities and makes intercession for us with groanings which cannot be uttered (Rom.8:26). When we enter our house which awaits us in heaven, "mortality" will be "swallowed up of life" (2 Cor.5:4).

If we now turn to Hebrews 11, we may be able to add one further feature that is encouraging to the Pilgrim. 2 Corinthians 5 arises out of what is said in 2 Corinthians 4:18, the first word of 2 Corinthians 5:1 being the logical connective "for":

> "While we look not at the things which are seen, but at the things which are not seen: for the things which are seen are temporal; but the things which are not seen are eternal".

Hebrews 11 which draws attention to the tent dwelling of Abraham in view of the city which hath foundations, opens with the words:

> "Now faith is the substance of things hoped for" (Heb.11:1).

The word *hupostases*, translated here "substance" is found in a Papyrus that has recently been examined to mean "the title deeds" to property. The believer, the moment he comes under the Passover Redemption of Christ, becomes a Pilgrim; this we have seen. Like Abraham, he is willing to be a sojourner, because he seeks a better, that is a heavenly country.

He has however many consolations to mitigate the groans that will escape him. He is assured that God also is sharing this Pilgrimage with him. He does not walk alone. Moreover, even though the body he now possesses is marked with frailty, and likened to a tent, which by its very nature is temporary and soon worn out, he carries with him throughout his pilgrimage "the title deeds" to a building of God, an house not made with hands, eternal in the heavens. In 2 Corinthians 5:5 we have, instead of the title deeds "the earnest of the Spirit".

Even though the members of the Body of Christ await the day of manifestation for the realization of their hope; even though they too are on a pilgrimage and have to endure hardness, they too are citizens of no mean city, for Philippians 3:20,21 says:

"Our conversation (*politeuma* — citizenship) is in heaven; from whence also we look for the Saviour, the Lord Jesus Christ: Who shall change our vile body (this body of humiliation) that it may be fashioned like unto His glorious body, according to the working whereby He is able even to subdue all things unto Himself".

"I nightly pitch my moving tent
A day's march nearer home".

****

Many more books and booklets from the pen of Charles Welch and other authors are also available.

* * *

In addition we have a large library of lectures and addresses on tape and cassette which may be purchased or obtained on loan.

* * *

Write for free catalogues to:

THE BEREAN PUBLISHING TRUST
52a Wilson Street, London EC2A 2ER
England